Poems fro

by Oliver Wendell Holmes

CONTENTS:

POEMS FROM OVER THE TEACUPS.

THE MOTHER'S SECRET

THE SECRET OF THE STARS

POEMS FROM OVER THE TEACUPS

TO THE ELEVEN LADIES

WHO PRESENTED ME WITH A SILVER LOVING CUP

ON THE TWENTY-NINTH OF AUGUST, M DCCC LXXXIX

"WHO gave this cup?" The secret thou wouldst steal

Its brimming flood forbids it to reveal:

No mortal's eye shall read it till he first

Cool the red throat of thirst.

If on the golden floor one draught remain,

Trust me, thy careful search will be in vain;

Not till the bowl is emptied shalt thou know

The names enrolled below.

Deeper than Truth lies buried in her well

Those modest names the graven letters spell

Hide from the sight; but wait, and thou shalt see

Who the good angels be

Whose bounty glistens in the beauteous gift

That friendly hands to loving lips shall lift

Turn the fair goblet when its floor is dry,--

Their names shall meet thine eye.

Count thou their number on the beads of Heaven

Alas! the clustered Pleiads are but seven;

Nay, the nine sister Muses are too few,--

The Graces must add two.

"For whom this gift?" For one who all too long

Clings to his bough among the groves of song;

Autumn's last leaf, that spreads its faded wing

To greet a second spring.

Dear friends, kind friends, whate'er the cup may hold,

Bathing its burnished depths, will change to gold

Its last bright drop let thirsty Maenads drain,

Its fragrance will remain.

Better love's perfume in the empty bowl

Than wine's nepenthe for the aching soul;

Sweeter than song that ever poet sung,

It makes an old heart young!

THE PEAU DE CHAGRIN OF STATE STREET

How beauteous is the bond

In the manifold array

Of its promises to pay,

While the eight per cent it gives

And the rate at which one lives

Correspond!

But at last the bough is bare

Where the coupons one by one

Through their ripening days have run,

And the bond, a beggar now,

Seeks investment anyhow,

Anywhere!

CACOETHES SCRIBENDI

IF all the trees in all the woods were men;

And each and every blade of grass a pen;

If every leaf on every shrub and tree

Turned to a sheet of foolscap; every sea

Were changed to ink, and all earth's living tribes

Had nothing else to do but act as scribes,

And for ten thousand ages, day and night,

The human race should write, and write, and write,

Till all the pens and paper were used up,

And the huge inkstand was an empty cup,

Still would the scribblers clustered round its brink

Call for more pens, more paper, and more ink.

THE ROSE AND THE FERN

LADY, life's sweetest lesson wouldst thou learn,

Come thou with me to Love's enchanted bower

High overhead the trellised roses burn;

Beneath thy feet behold the feathery fern,--

A leaf without a flower.

What though the rose leaves fall? They still are sweet,

And have been lovely in their beauteous prime,

While the bare frond seems ever to repeat,

"For us no bud, no blossom, wakes to greet

The joyous flowering time!"

Heed thou the lesson. Life has leaves to tread

And flowers to cherish; summer round thee glows;

Wait not till autumn's fading robes are shed,

But while its petals still are burning red

Gather life's full-blown rose!

I LIKE YOU AND I LOVE YOU

I LIKE YOU Met I LOVE You, face to face;

The path was narrow, and they could not pass.

I LIKE YOU smiled; I LOVE YOU cried, Alas!

And so they halted for a little space.

"Turn thou and go before," I LOVE YOU said,

"Down the green pathway, bright with many a flower;

Deep in the valley, lo! my bridal bower

Awaits thee." But I LIKE YOU shook his head.

Then while they lingered on the span-wide shelf

That shaped a pathway round the rocky ledge,

I LIKE You bared his icy dagger's edge,

And first he slew I LOVE You,--then himself.

LA MAISON D'OR

(BAR HARBOR)

FROM this fair home behold on either side

The restful mountains or the restless sea

So the warm sheltering walls of life divide

Time and its tides from still eternity.

Look on the waves: their stormy voices teach

That not on earth may toil and struggle cease.

Look on the mountains: better far than speech

Their silent promise of eternal peace.

TOO YOUNG FOR LOVE

Too young for love?

Ah, say not so!

Tell reddening rose-buds not to blow

Wait not for spring to pass away,--

Love's summer months begin with May!

Too young for love?

Ah, say not so!

Too young? Too young?

Ah, no! no! no!

Too young for love?

Ah, say not so,

To practise all love learned in May.

June soon will come with lengthened day

While daisies bloom and tulips glow!

Too young for love?

Ah, say not so!

Too young? Too young?

Ah, no! no! no

THE BROOMSTICK TRAIN; OR,

THE RETURN OF THE WITCHES

LOOK out! Look out, boys! Clear the track!

The witches are here! They've all come back!

They hanged them high,--No use! No use!

What cares a witch for a hangman's noose?

They buried them deep, but they wouldn't lie still,

For cats and witches are hard to kill;

They swore they shouldn't and wouldn't die,--

Books said they did, but they lie! they lie!

A couple of hundred years, or so,

They had knocked about in the world below,

When an Essex Deacon dropped in to call,

And a homesick feeling seized them all;

For he came from a place they knew full well,

And many a tale he had to tell.

They longed to visit the haunts of men,

To see the old dwellings they knew again,

And ride on their broomsticks all around

Their wide domain of unhallowed ground.

In Essex county there's many a roof

Well known to him of the cloven hoof;

The small square windows are full in view

Which the midnight hags went sailing through,

On their well-trained broomsticks mounted high,

Seen like shadows against the sky;

Crossing the track of owls and bats,

Hugging before them their coal-black cats.

Well did they know, those gray old wives,

The sights we see in our daily drives

Shimmer of lake and shine of sea,

Browne's bare hill with its lonely tree,

(It was n't then as we see it now,

With one scant scalp-lock to shade its brow;)

Dusky nooks in the Essex woods,

Dark, dim, Dante-like solitudes,

Where the tree-toad watches the sinuous snake

Glide through his forests of fern and brake;

Ipswich River; its old stone bridge;

Far off Andover's Indian Ridge,

And many a scene where history tells

Some shadow of bygone terror dwells,--

Of "Norman's Woe" with its tale of dread,

Of the Screeching Woman of Marblehead,

(The fearful story that turns men pale

Don't bid me tell it,--my speech would fail.)

Who would not, will not, if he can,

Bathe in the breezes of fair Cape Ann,--

Rest in the bowers her bays enfold,

Loved by the sachems and squaws of old?

Home where the white magnolias bloom,

Sweet with the bayberry's chaste perfume,

Hugged by the woods and kissed by the sea!

Where is the Eden like to thee?

For that "couple of hundred years, or so,"

There had been no peace in the world below;

The witches still grumbling, "It is n't fair;

Come, give us a taste of the upper air!

We 've had enough of your sulphur springs,

And the evil odor that round them clings;

We long for a drink that is cool and nice,--

Great buckets of water with Wenham ice;

We've served you well up-stairs, you know;

You 're a good old--fellow--come, let us go!"

I don't feel sure of his being good,

But he happened to be in a pleasant mood,--

As fiends with their skins full sometimes are,--

(He'd been drinking with "roughs" at a Boston bar.)

So what does he do but up and shout

To a graybeard turnkey, "Let 'em out!"

To mind his orders was all he knew;

The gates swung open, and out they flew.

"Where are our broomsticks?" the beldams cried.

"Here are your broomsticks," an imp replied.

"They 've been in--the place you know--so long

They smell of brimstone uncommon strong;

But they've gained by being left alone,--

Just look, and you'll see how tall they've grown."

"And where is my cat?" a vixen squalled.

"Yes, where are our cats?" the witches bawled,

And began to call them all by name

As fast as they called the cats, they came

There was bob-tailed Tommy and long-tailed Tim,

And wall-eyed Jacky and green-eyed Jim,

And splay-foot Benny and slim-legged Beau,

And Skinny and Squally, and Jerry and Joe,

And many another that came at call,--

It would take too long to count them all.

All black,--one could hardly tell which was which,

But every cat knew his own old witch;

And she knew hers as hers knew her,--

Ah, didn't they curl their tails and purr!

No sooner the withered hags were free

Than out they swarmed for a midnight spree;

I couldn't tell all they did in rhymes,

But the Essex people had dreadful times.

The Swampscott fishermen still relate

How a strange sea-monster stole their bait;

How their nets were tangled in loops and knots,

And they found dead crabs in their lobster-pots.

Poor Danvers grieved for her blasted crops,

And Wilmington mourned over mildewed hops.

A blight played havoc with Beverly beans,--

It was all the work of those hateful queans!

A dreadful panic began at "Pride's,"

Where the witches stopped in their midnight rides,

And there rose strange rumors and vague alarms

'Mid the peaceful dwellers at Beverly Farms.

Now when the Boss of the Beldams found

That without his leave they were ramping round,

He called,--they could hear him twenty miles,

From Chelsea beach to the Misery Isles;

The deafest old granny knew his tone

Without the trick of the telephone.

"Come here, you witches! Come here!" says he,--

"At your games of old, without asking me!

I'll give you a little job to do

That will keep you stirring, you godless crew!"

They came, of course, at their master's call,

The witches, the broomsticks, the cats, and all;

He led the hags to a railway train

The horses were trying to drag in vain.

"Now, then," says he, "you've had your fun,

And here are the cars you've got to run.

The driver may just unhitch his team,

We don't want horses, we don't want steam;

You may keep your old black cats to hug,

But the loaded train you've got to lug."

Since then on many a car you 'll see

A broomstick plain as plain can be;

On every stick there's a witch astride,--

The string you see to her leg is tied.

She will do a mischief if she can,

But the string is held by a careful man,

And whenever the evil-minded witch

Would cut some caper, he gives a twitch.

As for the hag, you can't see her,

But hark! you can hear her black cat's purr,

And now and then, as a car goes by,

You may catch a gleam from her wicked eye.

Often you've looked on a rushing train,

But just what moved it was not so plain.

It couldn't be those wires above,

For they could neither pull nor shove;

Where was the motor that made it go

You couldn't guess, but now you know.

Remember my rhymes when you ride again

On the rattling rail by the broomstick train!

TARTARUS

WHILE in my simple gospel creed

That "God is Love" so plain I read,

Shall dreams of heathen birth affright

My pathway through the coming night?

Ah, Lord of life, though spectres pale

Fill with their threats the shadowy vale,

With Thee my faltering steps to aid,

How can I dare to be afraid?

Shall mouldering page or fading scroll

Outface the charter of the soul?

Shall priesthood's palsied arm protect

The wrong our human hearts reject,

And smite the lips whose shuddering cry

Proclaims a cruel creed a lie?

The wizard's rope we disallow

Was justice once,--is murder now!

Is there a world of blank despair,

And dwells the Omnipresent there?

Does He behold with smile serene

The shows of that unending scene,

Where sleepless, hopeless anguish lies,

And, ever dying, never dies?

Say, does He hear the sufferer's groan,

And is that child of wrath his own?

O mortal, wavering in thy trust,

Lift thy pale forehead from the dust!

The mists that cloud thy darkened eyes

Fade ere they reach the o'erarching skies

When the blind heralds of despair

Would bid thee doubt a Father's care,

Look up from earth, and read above

On heaven's blue tablet, GOD IS LOVE!

AT THE TURN OF THE ROAD

THE glory has passed from the goldenrod's plume,

The purple-hued asters still linger in bloom

The birch is bright yellow, the sumachs are red,

The maples like torches aflame overhead.

But what if the joy of the summer is past,

And winter's wild herald is blowing his blast?

For me dull November is sweeter than May,

For my love is its sunshine,--she meets me to-day!

Will she come? Will the ring-dove return to her nest?

Will the needle swing back from the east or the west?

At the stroke of the hour she will be at her gate;

A friend may prove laggard,--love never comes late.

Do I see her afar in the distance? Not yet.

Too early! Too early! She could not forget!

When I cross the old bridge where the brook overflowed,

She will flash full in sight at the turn of the road.

I pass the low wall where the ivy entwines;

I tread the brown pathway that leads through the pines;

I haste by the boulder that lies in the field,

Where her promise at parting was lovingly sealed.

Will she come by the hillside or round through the wood?

Will she wear her brown dress or her mantle and hood?

The minute draws near,--but her watch may go wrong;

My heart will be asking, What keeps her so long?

Why doubt for a moment? More shame if I do!

Why question? Why tremble? Are angels more true?

She would come to the lover who calls her his own

Though she trod in the track of a whirling cyclone!

I crossed the old bridge ere the minute had passed.

I looked: lo! my Love stood before me at last.

Her eyes, how they sparkled, her cheeks, how they glowed,

As we met, face to face, at the turn of the road!

IN VITA MINERVA

VEX not the Muse with idle prayers,--

She will not hear thy call;

She steals upon thee unawares,

Or seeks thee not at all.

Soft as the moonbeams when they sought

Endymion's fragrant bower,

She parts the whispering leaves of thought

To show her full-blown flower.

For thee her wooing hour has passed,

The singing birds have flown,

And winter comes with icy blast

To chill thy buds unblown.

Yet, though the woods no longer thrill

As once their arches rung,

Sweet echoes hover round thee still

Of songs thy summer sung.

Live in thy past; await no more

The rush of heaven-sent wings;

Earth still has music left in store

While Memory sighs and sings.

READINGS OVER THE TEACUPS

FIVE STORIES AND A SEQUEL

TO MY OLD READERS

You know "The Teacups," that congenial set

Which round the Teapot you have often met;

The grave DICTATOR, him you knew of old,--

Knew as the shepherd of another fold

Grayer he looks, less youthful, but the same

As when you called him by a different name.

Near him the MISTRESS, whose experienced skill

Has taught her duly every cup to fill;

"Weak;" "strong;" "cool;" "lukewarm; "hot as you can pour;" "No sweetening;" "sugared;" "two lumps;" "one lump more."

Next, the PROFESSOR, whose scholastic phrase

At every turn the teacher's tongue betrays,

Trying so hard to make his speech precise

The captious listener finds it overnice.

Nor be forgotten our ANNEXES twain,

Nor HE, the owner of the squinting brain,

Which, while its curious fancies we pursue,

Oft makes us question, "Are we crack-brained too?"

Along the board our growing list extends,

As one by one we count our clustering friends,--

The youthful DOCTOR waiting for his share

Of fits and fevers when his crown gets bare;

In strong, dark lines our square-nibbed pen should draw

The lordly presence of the MAN OF LAW;

Our bashful TUTOR claims a humbler place,

A lighter touch, his slender form to trace.

Mark the fair lady he is seated by,--

Some say he is her lover,--some deny,--

Watch them together,--time alone can show

If dead-ripe friendship turns to love or no.

Where in my list of phrases shall I seek

The fitting words of NUMBER FIVE to speak?

Such task demands a readier pen than mine,--

What if I steal the Tutor's Valentine?

Why should I call her gracious, winning, fair?

Why with the loveliest of her sex compare?

Those varied charms have many a Muse inspired,--

At last their worn superlatives have tired;

Wit, beauty, sweetness, each alluring grace,

All these in honeyed verse have found their place;

I need them not,--two little words I find

Which hold them all in happiest form combined;

No more with baffled language will I strive,--

All in one breath I utter: Number Five!

Now count our teaspoons--if you care to learn

How many tinkling cups were served in turn,--

Add all together, you will find them ten,--

Our young MUSICIAN joined us now and then.

Our bright DELILAH you must needs recall,

The comely handmaid, youngest of us all;

Need I remind you how the little maid

Came at a pinch to our Professor's aid,--

Trimmed his long locks with unrelenting shears

And eased his looks of half a score of years?

Sometimes, at table, as you well must know,

The stream of talk will all at once run low,

The air seems smitten with a sudden chill,

The wit grows silent and the gossip still;

This was our poet's chance, the hour of need,

When rhymes and stories we were used to read.

One day a whisper round the teacups stole,--

"No scrap of paper in the silver bowl!"

(Our "poet's corner" may I not expect

My kindly reader still may recollect?)

"What! not a line to keep our souls alive?"

Spoke in her silvery accents Number Five.

"No matter, something we must find to read,--

Find it or make it,--yes, we must indeed!

Now I remember I have seen at times

Some curious stories in a book of rhymes,--

How certain secrets, long in silence sealed,

In after days were guessed at or revealed.

Those stories, doubtless, some of you must know,--

They all were written many a year ago;

But an old story, be it false or true,

Twice told, well told, is twice as good as new;

Wait but three sips and I will go myself,

And fetch the book of verses from its shelf."

No time was lost in finding what she sought,--

Gone but one moment,--lo! the book is brought.

"Now, then, Professor, fortune has decreed

That you, this evening, shall be first to read,--

Lucky for us that listen, for in fact

Who reads this poem must know how to act."

Right well she knew that in his greener age

He had a mighty hankering for the stage.

The patient audience had not long to wait;

Pleased with his chance, he smiled and took the bait;

Through his wild hair his coaxing fingers ran,--

He spread the page before him and began.

THE BANKER'S SECRET

THE Banker's dinner is the stateliest feast

The town has heard of for a year, at least;

The sparry lustres shed their broadest blaze,

Damask and silver catch and spread the rays;

The florist's triumphs crown the daintier spoil

Won from the sea, the forest, or the soil;

The steaming hot-house yields its largest pines,

The sunless vaults unearth their oldest wines;

With one admiring look the scene survey,

And turn a moment from the bright display.

Of all the joys of earthly pride or power,

What gives most life, worth living, in an hour?

When Victory settles on the doubtful fight

And the last foeman wheels in panting flight,

No thrill like this is felt beneath the sun;

Life's sovereign moment is a battle won.

But say what next? To shape a Senate's choice,

By the strong magic of the master's voice;

To ride the stormy tempest of debate

That whirls the wavering fortunes of the state.

Third in the list, the happy lover's prize

Is won by honeyed words from women's eyes.

If some would have it first instead of third,

So let it be,--I answer not a word.

The fourth,--sweet readers, let the thoughtless half

Have its small shrug and inoffensive laugh;

Let the grave quarter wear its virtuous frown,

The stern half-quarter try to scowl us down;

But the last eighth, the choice and sifted few,

Will hear my words, and, pleased, confess them true.

Among the great whom Heaven has made to shine,

How few have learned the art of arts,--to dine!

Nature, indulgent to our daily need,

Kind-hearted mother! taught us all to feed;

But the chief art,--how rarely Nature flings

This choicest gift among her social kings

Say, man of truth, has life a brighter hour

Than waits the chosen guest who knows his power?

He moves with ease, itself an angel charm,--

Lifts with light touch my lady's jewelled arm,

Slides to his seat, half leading and half led,

Smiling but quiet till the grace is said,

Then gently kindles, while by slow degrees

Creep softly out the little arts that please;

Bright looks, the cheerful language of the eye,

The neat, crisp question and the gay reply,--

Talk light and airy, such as well may pass

Between the rested fork and lifted glass;--

With play like this the earlier evening flies,

Till rustling silks proclaim the ladies rise.

His hour has come,--he looks along the chairs,

As the Great Duke surveyed his iron squares.

That's the young traveller,--is n't much to show,--

Fast on the road, but at the table slow.

Next him,--you see the author in his look,--

His forehead lined with wrinkles like a book,--

Wrote the great history of the ancient Huns,--

Holds back to fire among the heavy guns.

Oh, there's our poet seated at his side,

Beloved of ladies, soft, cerulean-eyed.

Poets are prosy in their common talk,

As the fast trotters, for the most part, walk.

And there's our well-dressed gentleman, who sits,

By right divine, no doubt, among the wits,

Who airs his tailor's patterns when he walks,

The man that often speaks, but never talks.

Why should he talk, whose presence lends a grace

To every table where he shows his face?

He knows the manual of the silver fork,

Can name his claret--if he sees the cork,--

Remark that "White-top" was considered fine,

But swear the "Juno" is the better wine;--

Is not this talking? Ask Quintilian's rules;

If they say No, the town has many fools.

Pause for a moment,--for our eyes behold

The plain unsceptred king, the man of gold,

The thrice illustrious threefold millionnaire;

Mark his slow-creeping, dead, metallic stare;

His eyes, dull glimmering, like the balance-pan

That weighs its guinea as he weighs his man.

Who's next? An artist in a satin tie

Whose ample folds defeat the curious eye.

And there 's the cousin,--must be asked, you know,--

Looks like a spinster at a baby-show.

Hope he is cool,--they set him next the door,--

And likes his place, between the gap and bore.

Next comes a Congressman, distinguished guest

We don't count him,--they asked him with the rest;

And then some white cravats, with well-shaped ties,

And heads above them which their owners prize.

Of all that cluster round the genial board,

Not one so radiant as the banquet's lord.

Some say they fancy, but they know not why,

A shade of trouble brooding in his eye,

Nothing, perhaps,--the rooms are overhot,--

Yet see his cheek,--the dull-red burning spot,--

Taste the brown sherry which he does not pass,--

Ha! That is brandy; see him fill his glass!

But not forgetful of his feasting friends,

To each in turn some lively word he sends;

See how he throws his baited lines about,

And plays his men as anglers play their trout.

A question drops among the listening crew

And hits the traveller, pat on Timbuctoo.

We're on the Niger, somewhere near its source,--

Not the least hurry, take the river's course

Through Kissi, Foota, Kankan, Bammakoo,

Bambarra, Sego, so to Timbuctoo,

Thence down to Youri;--stop him if we can,

We can't fare worse,--wake up the Congressman!

The Congressman, once on his talking legs,

Stirs up his knowledge to its thickest dregs;

Tremendous draught for dining men to quaff!

Nothing will choke him but a purpling laugh.

A word,--a shout,--a mighty roar,--'t is done;

Extinguished; lassoed by a treacherous pun.

A laugh is priming to the loaded soul;

The scattering shots become a steady roll,

Broke by sharp cracks that run along the line,

The light artillery of the talker's wine.

The kindling goblets flame with golden dews,

The hoarded flasks their tawny fire diffuse,

And the Rhine's breast-milk gushes cold and bright,

Pale as the moon and maddening as her light;

With crimson juice the thirsty southern sky

Sucks from the hills where buried armies lie,

So that the dreamy passion it imparts

Is drawn from heroes' bones and lovers' hearts.

But lulls will come; the flashing soul transmits

Its gleams of light in alternating fits.

The shower of talk that rattled down amain

Ends in small patterings like an April's rain;

With the dry sticks all bonfires are begun;

Bring the first fagot, proser number one

The voices halt; the game is at a stand;

Now for a solo from the master-hand

'T is but a story,--quite a simple thing,--

An aria touched upon a single string,

But every accent comes with such a grace

The stupid servants listen in their place,

Each with his waiter in his lifted hands,

Still as a well-bred pointer when he stands.

A query checks him: "Is he quite exact?"

(This from a grizzled, square-jawed man of fact.)

The sparkling story leaves him to his fate,

Crushed by a witness, smothered with a date,

As a swift river, sown with many a star,

Runs brighter, rippling on a shallow bar.

The smooth divine suggests a graver doubt;

A neat quotation bowls the parson out;

Then, sliding gayly from his own display,

He laughs the learned dulness all away.

So, with the merry tale and jovial song,

The jocund evening whirls itself along,

Till the last chorus shrieks its loud encore,

And the white neckcloths vanish through the door.

One savage word!--The menials know its tone,

And slink away; the master stands alone.

Well played, by ------"; breathe not what were best unheard; His goblet shivers while he speaks the word,--

"If wine tells truth,--and so have said the wise,--

It makes me laugh to think how brandy lies!

Bankrupt to-morrow,--millionnaire to-day,--

The farce is over,--now begins the play!"

The spring he touches lets a panel glide;

An iron closet harks beneath the slide,

Bright with such treasures as a search might bring

From the deep pockets of a truant king.

Two diamonds, eyeballs of a god of bronze,

Bought from his faithful priest, a pious bonze;

A string of brilliants; rubies, three or four;

Bags of old coin and bars of virgin ore;

A jewelled poniard and a Turkish knife,

Noiseless and useful if we come to strife.

Gone! As a pirate flies before the wind,

And not one tear for all he leaves behind

From all the love his better years have known

Fled like a felon,--ah! but not alone!

The chariot flashes through a lantern's glare,--

Oh the wild eyes! the storm of sable hair!

Still to his side the broken heart will cling,--

The bride of shame, the wife without the ring

Hark, the deep oath,--the wail of frenzied woe,--

Lost! lost to hope of Heaven and peace below!

He kept his secret; but the seed of crime

Bursts of itself in God's appointed time.

The lives he wrecked were scattered far and wide;

One never blamed nor wept,--she only died.

None knew his lot, though idle tongues would say

He sought a lonely refuge far away,

And there, with borrowed name and altered mien,

He died unheeded, as he lived unseen.

The moral market had the usual chills

Of Virtue suffering from protested bills;

The White Cravats, to friendship's memory true,

Sighed for the past, surveyed the future too;

Their sorrow breathed in one expressive line,--

"Gave pleasant dinners; who has got his wine?"

. . . .

The reader paused,--the Teacups knew his ways,--

He, like the rest, was not averse to praise.

Voices and hands united; every one

Joined in approval: "Number Three, well done!"

"Now for the Exile's story; if my wits

Are not at fault, his curious record fits

Neatly as sequel to the tale we've heard;

Not wholly wild the fancy, nor absurd

That this our island hermit well might be

That story's hero, fled from over sea.

Come, Number Seven, we would not have you strain

The fertile powers of that inventive brain.

Read us 'The Exile's Secret'; there's enough

Of dream-like fiction and fantastic stuff

In the strange web of mystery that invests

The lonely isle where sea birds build their nests."

"Lies! naught but lies!" so Number Seven began,--

No harm was known of that secluded man.

He lived alone,--who would n't if he might,

And leave the rogues and idiots out of sight?

A foolish story,--still, I'll do my best,--

The house was real,--don't believe the rest.

How could a ruined dwelling last so long

Without its legends shaped in tale and song?

Who was this man of whom they tell the lies?

Perhaps--why not?--NAPOLEON! in disguise,--

So some said, kidnapped from his ocean coop,

Brought to this island in a coasting sloop,--

Meanwhile a sham Napoleon in his place

Played Nap. and saved Sir Hudson from disgrace.

Such was one story; others used to say,

"No,--not Napoleon,--it was Marshal Ney."

"Shot?" Yes, no doubt, but not with balls of lead,

But balls of pith that never shoot folks dead.

He wandered round, lived South for many a year,

At last came North and fixed his dwelling here.

Choose which you will of all the tales that pile

Their mingling fables on the tree-crowned isle.

Who wrote this modest version I suppose

That truthful Teacup, our Dictator, knows;

Made up of various legends, it would seem,

The sailor's yarn, the crazy poet's dream.

Such tales as this, by simple souls received,

At first are stared at and at last believed;

From threads like this the grave historians try

To weave their webs, and never know they lie.

Hear, then, the fables that have gathered round

The lonely home an exiled stranger found.

THE EXILE'S SECRET

YE that have faced the billows and the spray

Of good St. Botolph's island-studded bay,

As from the gliding bark your eye has scanned

The beaconed rocks, the wave-girt hills of sand,

Have ye not marked one elm-o'ershadowed isle,

Round as the dimple chased in beauty's smile,--

A stain of verdure on an azure field,

Set like a jewel in a battered shield?

Fixed in the narrow gorge of Ocean's path,

Peaceful it meets him in his hour of wrath;

When the mailed Titan, scourged by hissing gales,

Writhes in his glistening coat of clashing scales,

The storm-beat island spreads its tranquil green,

Calm as an emerald on an angry queen.

So fair when distant should be fairer near;

A boat shall waft us from the outstretched pier.

The breeze blows fresh; we reach the island's edge,

Our shallop rustling through the yielding sedge.

No welcome greets us on the desert isle;

Those elms, far-shadowing, hide no stately pile

Yet these green ridges mark an ancient road;

And to! the traces of a fair abode;

The long gray line that marks a garden-wall,

And heaps of fallen beams,--fire-branded all.

Who sees unmoved, a ruin at his feet,

The lowliest home where human hearts have beat?

Its hearthstone, shaded with the bistre stain

A century's showery torrents wash in vain;

Its starving orchard, where the thistle blows

And mossy trunks still mark the broken rows;

Its chimney-loving poplar, oftenest seen

Next an old roof, or where a roof has been;

Its knot-grass, plantain,--all the social weeds,

Man's mute companions, following where he leads;

Its dwarfed, pale flowers, that show their straggling heads, Sown by the wind from grass-choked garden-beds;

Its woodbine, creeping where it used to climb;

Its roses, breathing of the olden time;

All the poor shows the curious idler sees,

As life's thin shadows waste by slow degrees,

Till naught remains, the saddening tale to tell,

Save home's last wrecks,--the cellar and the well?

And whose the home that strews in black decay

The one green-glowing island of the bay?

Some dark-browed pirate's, jealous of the fate

That seized the strangled wretch of "Nix's Mate"?

Some forger's, skulking in a borrowed name,

Whom Tyburn's dangling halter yet may claim?

Some wan-eyed exile's, wealth and sorrow's heir,

Who sought a lone retreat for tears and prayer?

Some brooding poet's, sure of deathless fame,

Had not his epic perished in the flame?

Or some gray wooer's, whom a girlish frown

Chased from his solid friends and sober town?

Or some plain tradesman's, fond of shade and ease,

Who sought them both beneath these quiet trees?

Why question mutes no question can unlock,

Dumb as the legend on the Dighton rock?

One thing at least these ruined heaps declare,--

They were a shelter once; a man lived there.

But where the charred and crumbling records fail,

Some breathing lips may piece the half-told tale;

No man may live with neighbors such as these,

Though girt with walls of rock and angry seas,

And shield his home, his children, or his wife,

His ways, his means, his vote, his creed, his life,

From the dread sovereignty of Ears and Eyes

And the small member that beneath them lies.

They told strange things of that mysterious man;

Believe who will, deny them such as can;

Why should we fret if every passing sail

Had its old seaman talking on the rail?

The deep-sunk schooner stuffed with Eastern lime,

Slow wedging on, as if the waves were slime;

The knife-edged clipper with her ruffled spars,

The pawing steamer with her inane of stars,

The bull-browed galliot butting through the stream,

The wide-sailed yacht that slipped along her beam,

The deck-piled sloops, the pinched chebacco-boats,

The frigate, black with thunder-freighted throats,

All had their talk about the lonely man;

And thus, in varying phrase, the story ran.

His name had cost him little care to seek,

Plain, honest, brief, a decent name to speak,

Common, not vulgar, just the kind that slips

With least suggestion from a stranger's lips.

His birthplace England, as his speech might show,

Or his hale cheek, that wore the red-streak's glow;

His mouth sharp-moulded; in its mirth or scorn

There came a flash as from the milky corn,

When from the ear you rip the rustling sheath,

And the white ridges show their even teeth.

His stature moderate, but his strength confessed,

In spite of broadcloth, by his ample breast;

Full-armed, thick-handed; one that had been strong,

And might be dangerous still, if things went wrong.

He lived at ease beneath his elm-trees' shade,

Did naught for gain, yet all his debts were paid;

Rich, so 't was thought, but careful of his store;

Had all he needed, claimed to have no more.

But some that lingered round the isle at night

Spoke of strange stealthy doings in their sight;

Of creeping lonely visits that he made

To nooks and corners, with a torch and spade.

Some said they saw the hollow of a cave;

One, given to fables, swore it was a grave;

Whereat some shuddered, others boldly cried,

Those prowling boatmen lied, and knew they lied.

They said his house was framed with curious cares,

Lest some old friend might enter unawares;

That on the platform at his chamber's door

Hinged a loose square that opened through the floor;

Touch the black silken tassel next the bell,

Down, with a crash, the flapping trap-door fell;

Three stories deep the falling wretch would strike,

To writhe at leisure on a boarder's pike.

By day armed always; double-armed at night,

His tools lay round him; wake him such as might.

A carbine hung beside his India fan,

His hand could reach a Turkish ataghan;

Pistols, with quaint-carved stocks and barrels gilt,

Crossed a long dagger with a jewelled hilt;

A slashing cutlass stretched along the bed;--

All this was what those lying boatmen said.

Then some were full of wondrous stories told

Of great oak chests and cupboards full of gold;

Of the wedged ingots and the silver bars

That cost old pirates ugly sabre-scars;

How his laced wallet often would disgorge

The fresh-faced guinea of an English George,

Or sweated ducat, palmed by Jews of yore,

Or double Joe, or Portuguese moidore;

And how his finger wore a rubied ring

Fit for the white-necked play-girl of a king.

But these fine legends, told with staring eyes,

Met with small credence from the old and wise.

Why tell each idle guess, each whisper vain?

Enough : the scorched and cindered beams remain.

He came, a silent pilgrim to the West,

Some old-world mystery throbbing in his breast;

Close to the thronging mart he dwelt alone;

He lived; he died. The rest is all unknown.

Stranger, whose eyes the shadowy isle survey,

As the black steamer dashes through the bay,

Why ask his buried secret to divine?

He was thy brother; speak, and tell us thine!

. . . .

Silence at first, a kind of spell-bound pause;

Then all the Teacups tinkled their applause;

When that was hushed no sound the stillness broke

Till once again the soft-voiced lady spoke:

"The Lover's Secret,--surely that must need

The youngest voice our table holds to read.

Which of our two 'Annexes' shall we choose?

Either were charming, neither will refuse;

But choose we must,--what better can we do

Than take the younger of the youthful two?"

True to the primal instinct of her sex,

"Why, that means me," half whispered each Annex.

"What if it does?" the voiceless question came,

That set those pale New England cheeks aflame;

"Our old-world scholar may have ways to teach

Of Oxford English, Britain's purest speech,--

She shall be youngest,--youngest for to-day,--

Our dates we'll fix hereafter as we may;

All rights reserved,--the words we know so well,

That guard the claims of books which never sell."

The British maiden bowed a pleased assent,

Her two long ringlets swinging as she bent;

The glistening eyes her eager soul looked through

Betrayed her lineage in their Saxon blue.

Backward she flung each too obtrusive curl

And thus began,--the rose-lipped English girl.

THE LOVER'S SECRET

WHAT ailed young Lucius? Art had vainly tried

To guess his ill, and found herself defied.

The Augur plied his legendary skill;

Useless; the fair young Roman languished still.

His chariot took him every cloudless day

Along the Pincian Hill or Appian Way;

They rubbed his wasted limbs with sulphurous oil,

Oozed from the far-off Orient's heated soil;

They led him tottering down the steamy path

Where bubbling fountains filled the thermal bath;

Borne in his litter to Egeria's cave,

They washed him, shivering, in her icy wave.

They sought all curious herbs and costly stones,

They scraped the moss that grew on dead men's bones,

They tried all cures the votive tablets taught,

Scoured every place whence healing drugs were brought,

O'er Thracian hills his breathless couriers ran,

His slaves waylaid the Syrian caravan.

At last a servant heard a stranger speak

A new chirurgeon's name; a clever Greek,

Skilled in his art; from Pergamus he came

To Rome but lately; GALEN was the name.

The Greek was called: a man with piercing eyes,

Who must be cunning, and who might be wise.

He spoke but little,--if they pleased, he said,

He 'd wait awhile beside the sufferer's bed.

So by his side he sat, serene and calm,

His very accents soft as healing balm;

Not curious seemed, but every movement spied,

His sharp eyes searching where they seemed to glide;

Asked a few questions,--what he felt, and where?

"A pain just here," "A constant beating there."

Who ordered bathing for his aches and ails?

"Charmis, the water-doctor from Marseilles."

What was the last prescription in his case?

"A draught of wine with powdered chrysoprase."

Had he no secret grief he nursed alone?

A pause; a little tremor; answer,--"None."

Thoughtful, a moment, sat the cunning leech,

And muttered " Eros! " in his native speech.

In the broad atrium various friends await

The last new utterance from the lips of fate;

Men, matrons, maids, they talk the question o'er,

And, restless, pace the tessellated floor.

Not unobserved the youth so long had pined

By gentle-hearted dames and damsels kind;

One with the rest, a rich Patrician's pride,

The lady Hermia, called "the golden-eyed";

The same the old Proconsul fain must woo,

Whom, one dark night, a masked sicarius slew;

The same black Crassus over roughly pressed

To hear his suit,--the Tiber knows the rest.

(Crassus was missed next morning by his set;

Next week the fishers found him in their net.)

She with the others paced the ample hall,

Fairest, alas! and saddest of them all.

At length the Greek declared, with puzzled face,

Some strange enchantment mingled in the case,

And naught would serve to act as counter-charm

Save a warm bracelet from a maiden's arm.

Not every maiden's,--many might be tried;

Which not in vain, experience must decide.

Were there no damsels willing to attend

And do such service for a suffering friend?

The message passed among the waiting crowd,

First in a whisper, then proclaimed aloud.

Some wore no jewels; some were disinclined,

For reasons better guessed at than defined;

Though all were saints,--at least professed to be,--

The list all counted, there were named but three.

The leech, still seated by the patient's side,

Held his thin wrist, and watched him, eagle-eyed.

Aurelia first, a fair-haired Tuscan girl,

Slipped off her golden asp, with eyes of pearl.

His solemn head the grave physician shook;

The waxen features thanked her with a look.

Olympia next, a creature half divine,

Sprung from the blood of old Evander's line,

Held her white arm, that wore a twisted chain

Clasped with an opal-sheeny cymophane.

In vain, O daughter I said the baffled Greek.

The patient sighed the thanks he could not speak.

Last, Hermia entered; look, that sudden start!

The pallium heaves above his leaping heart;

The beating pulse, the cheek's rekindled flame,

Those quivering lips, the secret all proclaim.

The deep disease long throbbing in the breast,

The dread enchantment, all at once confessed!

The case was plain; the treatment was begun;

And Love soon cured the mischief he had done.

Young Love, too oft thy treacherous bandage slips

Down from the eyes it blinded to the lips!

Ask not the Gods, O youth, for clearer sight,

But the bold heart to plead thy cause aright.

And thou, fair maiden, when thy lovers sigh,

Suspect thy flattering ear, but trust thine eye;

And learn this secret from the tale of old

No love so true as love that dies untold.

. . . .

"Bravo, Annex!" they shouted, every one,--

"Not Mrs. Kemble's self had better done."

"Quite so," she stammered in her awkward way,--

Not just the thing, but something she must say.

The teaspoon chorus tinkled to its close

When from his chair the MAN OF LAW arose,

Called by her voice whose mandate all obeyed,

And took the open volume she displayed.

Tall, stately, strong, his form begins to own

Some slight exuberance in its central zone,--

That comely fulness of the growing girth

Which fifty summers lend the sons of earth.

A smooth, round disk about whose margin stray,

Above the temples, glistening threads of gray;

Strong, deep-cut grooves by toilsome decades wrought

On brow and mouth, the battle-fields of thought;

A voice that lingers in the listener's ear,

Grave, calm, far-reaching, every accent clear,--

(Those tones resistless many a foreman knew

That shaped their verdict ere the twelve withdrew;)

A statesman's forehead, athlete's throat and jaw,

Such the proud semblance of the Man of Law.

His eye just lighted on the printed leaf,

Held as a practised pleader holds his brief.

One whispered softly from behind his cup,

"He does not read,--his book is wrong side up!

He knows the story that it holds by heart,--

So like his own! How well he'll act his part!"

Then all were silent; not a rustling fan

Stirred the deep stillness as the voice began.

THE STATESMAN'S SECRET

WHO of all statesmen is his country's pride,

Her councils' prompter and her leaders' guide?

He speaks; the nation holds its breath to hear;

He nods, and shakes the sunset hemisphere.

Born where the primal fount of Nature springs

By the rude cradles of her throneless kings,

In his proud eye her royal signet flames,

By his own lips her Monarch she proclaims.

Why name his countless triumphs, whom to meet

Is to be famous, envied in defeat?

The keen debaters, trained to brawls and strife,

Who fire one shot, and finish with the knife,

Tried him but once, and, cowering in their shame,

Ground their hacked blades to strike at meaner game.

The lordly chief, his party's central stay,

Whose lightest word a hundred votes obey,

Found a new listener seated at his side,

Looked in his eye, and felt himself defied,

Flung his rash gauntlet on the startled floor,

Met the all-conquering, fought,--and ruled no more.

See where he moves, what eager crowds attend!

What shouts of thronging multitudes ascend!

If this is life,--to mark with every hour

The purple deepening in his robes of power,

To see the painted fruits of honor fall

Thick at his feet, and choose among them all,

To hear the sounds that shape his spreading name

Peal through the myriad organ-stops of fame,

Stamp the lone isle that spots the seaman's chart,

And crown the pillared glory of the mart,

To count as peers the few supremely wise

Who mark their planet in the angels' eyes,--

If this is life--

What savage man is he

Who strides alone beside the sounding sea?

Alone he wanders by the murmuring shore,

His thoughts as restless as the waves that roar;

Looks on the sullen sky as stormy-browed

As on the waves yon tempest-brooding cloud,

Heaves from his aching breast a wailing sigh,

Sad as the gust that sweeps the clouded sky.

Ask him his griefs; what midnight demons plough

The lines of torture on his lofty brow;

Unlock those marble lips, and bid them speak

The mystery freezing in his bloodless cheek.

His secret? Hid beneath a flimsy word;

One foolish whisper that ambition heard;

And thus it spake: "Behold yon gilded chair,

The world's one vacant throne,--thy plate is there!"

Ah, fatal dream! What warning spectres meet

In ghastly circle round its shadowy seat!

Yet still the Tempter murmurs in his ear

The maddening taunt he cannot choose but hear

"Meanest of slaves, by gods and men accurst,

He who is second when he might be first

Climb with bold front the ladder's topmost round,

Or chain thy creeping footsteps to the ground!"

Illustrious Dupe! Have those majestic eyes

Lost their proud fire for such a vulgar prize?

Art thou the last of all mankind to know

That party-fights are won by aiming low?

Thou, stamped by Nature with her royal sign,

That party-hirelings hate a look like thine?

Shake from thy sense the wild delusive dream

Without the purple, art thou not supreme?

And soothed by love unbought, thy heart shall own

A nation's homage nobler than its throne!

. . . .

Loud rang the plaudits; with them rose the thought,

"Would he had learned the lesson he has taught!"

Used to the tributes of the noisy crowd,

The stately speaker calmly smiled and bowed;

The fire within a flushing cheek betrayed,

And eyes that burned beneath their penthouse shade.

"The clock strikes ten, the hours are flying fast,--

Now, Number Five, we've kept you till the last!"

What music charms like those caressing tones

Whose magic influence every listener owns,--

Where all the woman finds herself expressed,

And Heaven's divinest effluence breathes confessed?

Such was the breath that wooed our ravished ears,

Sweet as the voice a dreaming vestal hears;

Soft as the murmur of a brooding dove,

It told the mystery of a mother's love.

THE MOTHER'S SECRET

How sweet the sacred legend--if unblamed

In my slight verse such holy things are named--

Of Mary's secret hours of hidden joy,

Silent, but pondering on her wondrous boy!

Ave, Maria! Pardon, if I wrong

Those heavenly words that shame my earthly song!

The choral host had closed the Angel's strain

Sung to the listening watch on Bethlehem's plain,

And now the shepherds, hastening on their way,

Sought the still hamlet where the Infant lay.

They passed the fields that gleaning Ruth toiled o'er,--

They saw afar the ruined threshing-floor

Where Moab's daughter, homeless and forlorn,

Found Boaz slumbering by his heaps of corn;

And some remembered how the holy scribe,

Skilled in the lore of every jealous tribe,

Traced the warm blood of Jesse's royal son

To that fair alien, bravely wooed and won.

So fared they on to seek the promised sign,

That marked the anointed heir of David's line.

At last, by forms of earthly semblance led,

They found the crowded inn, the oxen's shed.

No pomp was there, no glory shone around

On the coarse straw that strewed the reeking ground;

One dim retreat a flickering torch betrayed,--

In that poor cell the Lord of Life was laid

The wondering shepherds told their breathless tale

Of the bright choir that woke the sleeping vale;

Told how the skies with sudden glory flamed,

Told how the shining multitude proclaimed,

"Joy, joy to earth! Behold the hallowed morn

In David's city Christ the Lord is born!

'Glory to God!' let angels shout on high,

'Good-will to men!' the listening earth reply!"

They spoke with hurried words and accents wild;

Calm in his cradle slept the heavenly child.

No trembling word the mother's joy revealed,--

One sigh of rapture, and her lips were sealed;

Unmoved she saw the rustic train depart,

But kept their words to ponder in her heart.

Twelve years had passed; the boy was fair and tall,

Growing in wisdom, finding grace with all.

The maids of Nazareth, as they trooped to fill

Their balanced urns beside the mountain rill,

The gathered matrons, as they sat and spun,

Spoke in soft words of Joseph's quiet son.

No voice had reached the Galilean vale

Of star-led kings, or awe-struck shepherd's tale;

In the meek, studious child they only saw

The future Rabbi, learned in Israel's law.

Beyond the hills that girt the village green;

Save when at midnight, o'er the starlit sands,

Snatched from the steel of Herod's murdering bands,

A babe, close folded to his mother's breast,

Through Edom's wilds he sought the sheltering West.

Then Joseph spake: "Thy boy hath largely grown;

Weave him fine raiment, fitting to be shown;

Fair robes beseem the pilgrim, as the priest;

Goes he not with us to the holy feast?"

And Mary culled the flaxen fibres white;

Till eve she spun; she spun till morning light.

The thread was twined; its parting meshes through

From hand to hand her restless shuttle flew,

Till the full web was wound upon the beam;

Love's curious toil,--a vest without a seam!

They reach the Holy Place, fulfil the days

To solemn feasting given, and grateful praise.

At last they turn, and far Moriah's height

Melts in the southern sky and fades from sight.

All day the dusky caravan has flowed

In devious trails along the winding road;

(For many a step their homeward path attends,

And all the sons of Abraham are as friends.)

Evening has come,--the hour of rest and joy,--

Hush! Hush! That whisper,--"Where is Mary's boy?"

Oh, weary hour! Oh, aching days that passed

Filled with strange fears each wilder than the last,--

The soldier's lance, the fierce centurion's sword,

The crushing wheels that whirl some Roman lord,

The midnight crypt that sucks the captive's breath,

The blistering sun on Hinnom's vale of death!

Thrice on his cheek had rained the morning light;

Thrice on his lips the mildewed kiss of night,

Crouched by a sheltering column's shining plinth,

Or stretched beneath the odorous terebinth.

At last, in desperate mood, they sought once more

The Temple's porches, searched in vain before;

They found him seated with the ancient men,--

The grim old rufflers of the tongue and pen,--

Their bald heads glistening as they clustered near,

Their gray beards slanting as they turned to hear,

Lost in half-envious wonder and surprise

That lips so fresh should utter words so wise.

And Mary said,--as one who, tried too long,

Tells all her grief and half her sense of wrong,--

What is this thoughtless thing which thou hast done?

Lo, we have sought thee sorrowing, O my son!

Few words he spake, and scarce of filial tone,

Strange words, their sense a mystery yet unknown;

Then turned with them and left the holy hill,

To all their mild commands obedient still.

The tale was told to Nazareth's sober men,

And Nazareth's matrons told it oft again;

The maids retold it at the fountain's side,

The youthful shepherds doubted or denied;

It passed around among the listening friends,

With all that fancy adds and fiction lends,

Till newer marvels dimmed the young renown

Of Joseph's son, who talked the Rabbis down.

But Mary, faithful to its lightest word,

Kept in her heart the sayings she had heard,

Till the dread morning rent the Temple's veil,

And shuddering earth confirmed the wondrous tale.

Youth fades; love droops; the leaves of friendship fall

A mother's secret hope outlives them all.

. . . .

Hushed was the voice, but still its accents thrilled

The throbbing hearts its lingering sweetness filled.

The simple story which a tear repays

Asks not to share the noisy breath of praise.

A trance-like stillness,--scarce a whisper heard,

No tinkling teaspoon in its saucer stirred;

A deep-drawn sigh that would not be suppressed,

A sob, a lifted kerchief told the rest.

"Come now, Dictator," so the lady spoke,

"You too must fit your shoulder to the yoke;

You'll find there's something, doubtless, if you look,

To serve your purpose,--so, now take the book."

"Ah, my dear lady, you must know full well,

'Story, God bless you, I have none to tell.'

To those five stories which these pages hold

You all have listened,--every one is told.

There's nothing left to make you smile or weep,--

A few grave thoughts may work you off to sleep."

THE SECRET OF THE STARS

Is man's the only throbbing heart that hides

The silent spring that feeds its whispering tides?

Speak from thy caverns, mystery-breeding Earth,

Tell the half-hinted story of thy birth,

And calm the noisy champions who have thrown

The book of types against the book of stone!

Have ye not secrets, ye refulgent spheres,

No sleepless listener of the starlight hears?

In vain the sweeping equatorial pries

Through every world-sown corner of the skies,

To the far orb that so remotely strays

Our midnight darkness is its noonday blaze;

In vain the climbing soul of creeping man

Metes out the heavenly concave with a span,

Tracks into space the long-lost meteor's trail,

And weighs an unseen planet in the scale;

Still o'er their doubts the wan-eyed watchers sigh,

And Science lifts her still unanswered cry

"Are all these worlds, that speed their circling flight,

Dumb, vacant, soulless,--baubles of the night?

Warmed with God's smile and wafted by his breath,

To weave in ceaseless round the dance of Death?

Or rolls a sphere in each expanding zone,

Crowned with a life as varied as our own?"

Maker of earth and stars! If thou hast taught

By what thy voice hath spoke, thy hand hath wrought,

By all that Science proves, or guesses true,

More than thy poet dreamed, thy prophet knew,--

The heavens still bow in darkness at thy feet,

And shadows veil thy cloud-pavilioned seat!

Not for ourselves we ask thee to reveal

One awful word beneath the future's seal;

What thou shalt tell us, grant us strength to bear;

What thou withholdest is thy single care.

Not for ourselves; the present clings too fast,

Moored to the mighty anchors of the past;

But when, with angry snap, some cable parts,

The sound re-echoing in our startled hearts,--

When, through the wall that clasps the harbor round,

And shuts the raving ocean from its bound,

Shattered and rent by sacrilegious hands,

The first mad billow leaps upon the sands,--

Then to the Future's awful page we turn,

And what we question hardly dare to learn.

Still let us hope! for while we seem to tread

The time-worn pathway of the nations dead,

Though Sparta laughs at all our warlike deeds,

And buried Athens claims our stolen creeds,

Though Rome, a spectre on her broken throne,

Beholds our eagle and recalls her own,

Though England fling her pennons on the breeze

And reign before us Mistress of the seas,--

While calm-eyed History tracks us circling round

Fate's iron pillar where they all were bound,

Still in our path a larger curve she finds,

The spiral widening as the chain unwinds

Still sees new beacons crowned with brighter flame

Than the old watch-fires, like, but not the same

No shameless haste shall spot with bandit-crime

Our destined empire snatched before its time.

Wait,--wait, undoubting, for the winds have caught

From our bold speech the heritage of thought;

No marble form that sculptured truth can wear

Vies with the image shaped in viewless air;

And thought unfettered grows through speech to deeds,

As the broad forest marches in its seeds.

What though we perish ere the day is won?

Enough to see its glorious work begun!

The thistle falls before a trampling clown,

But who can chain the flying thistle-down?

Wait while the fiery seeds of freedom fly,

The prairie blazes when the grass is dry!

What arms might ravish, leave to peaceful arts,

Wisdom and love shall win the roughest hearts;

So shall the angel who has closed for man

The blissful garden since his woes began

Swing wide the golden portals of the West,

And Eden's secret stand at length confessed!

. . . .

The reader paused; in truth he thought it time,--

Some threatening signs accused the drowsy rhyme.

The Mistress nodded, the Professor dozed,

The two Annexes sat with eyelids closed,--

Not sleeping,--no! But when one shuts one's eyes,

That one hears better no one, sure, denies.

The Doctor whispered in Delilah's ear,

Or seemed to whisper, for their heads drew near.

Not all the owner's efforts could restrain

The wild vagaries of the squinting brain,--

Last of the listeners Number Five alone

The patient reader still could call his own.

"Teacups, arouse!" 'T was thus the spell I broke;

The drowsy started and the slumberers woke.

"The sleep I promised you have now enjoyed,

Due to your hour of labor well employed.

Swiftly the busy moments have been passed;

This, our first 'Teacups,' must not be our last.

Here, on this spot, now consecrated ground,

The Order of 'The Teacups' let us found!

By winter's fireside and in summer's bower

Still shall it claim its ever-welcome hour,

In distant regions where our feet may roam

The magic teapot find or make a home;

Long may its floods their bright infusion pour,

Till time and teacups both shall be no more!"

###

Made in the USA
Coppell, TX
08 September 2023

21357200R00044